ISTRIA

and Venice

A foodie heaven

David Linton

ISTRIA AND VENICE

A foodie heaven

David Linton

First published in November 2022

David Linton has asserted his rights under the Copyright, Design and Patents Act 1988 to be identified as author of this work.

ISBN: 9798363461651

Other books by David Linton

Around the World in 80 Countries
Travel Experiences of a Lifetime

Fuerteventura
A winter escape

Cloud Charts
Trading Success with the Ichimoku Technique

All rights reserved. No part of this work covered by the copyright hereon may be reproduced or reused in any form or by any means - graphic, electronic, or merchandised, including photocopying, recording, taping or information storage and retrieval systems -
without the written permission of the author.

Every effort has been made to obtain the necessary permissions with reference to copyright material, both illustrative. We apologise for any omissions in this respect and will be pleased to make appropriate acknowledgements in any future edition.

Edited by Chris Bird, Sarah Robinson, and Emily Glorney

To

Emily

for sharing this great adventure with me

'Istria, a country of Italy'

The New World of English Words Dictionary, 1663

Contents

Introduction	7
Venice Arrival	9
Day Two in Venice	17
Our last day in Venice	25
ISTRIA	31
About Istria	33
Opatija	35
Pula	43
Rovinj	45
Pazin	51
Poreč	53
Novigrad	57
Grožnjan	59
Piran, Slovenia	63
Last Thoughts	69
Guide Book Reviews	71

Introduction

A travel plan comes together

I was invited to speak at a conference taking place in May 2022 in Opatija, on the north Croatian coast. I'd seen some beautiful pictures of towns on the coast near there and welcomed the opportunity to travel after a couple of years of lockdowns during the Coronavirus pandemic, so I accepted the invitation.

I initially thought I might drive all the way down from the UK, taking in Venice, which I hadn't visited since my childhood. While staying with an old friend, Jane, in Mallorca, we visited a super smart shop in Palma called Rialto Living. It seemed like destiny calling. Jane spent ages wandering around the stylish, interior-designed warren of rooms, while I settled in at the book section. My eyes worked their way around a large wall of shelves full of brightly coloured coffee table travel books featuring iconic places. I have travelled widely and as my eyes followed the titles, I mentally ticked off the places I had been; nearly all of them. My gaze stopped on a book titled *Istria*. 'Istria? Where is Istria?', I thought. 'Sounds Italian, but I am not exactly sure where it is.' So, I pulled the book, by Paola Bacchia, off the shelf. The arty representation of a laden olive branch indicated it was a cookbook, and the strapline, *recipes and stories from the heart of Italy, Slovenia and Croatia*, gave some indication as to where the region of Istria was located but I was still struggling to picture the boundaries. On opening the book, a map of this heart-shaped region dangling down into the top of the Adriatic Sea presented itself. And there, on the top eastern corner of the map, was Opatija, the town where my conference was being held.

I found myself getting lost in this book and the impatience I'd felt waiting for Jane, who was seemingly inspecting every item in this interior design Mecca, disappeared. Skimming through all the pages it was quicky becoming clear that Istria is a region of stunning scenery and also something of a foodie heaven. Truffles, olive oil, fresh seafood, fine wines, and many other foods of clearly fine providence, adorned the pages of this beautiful book. I was now salivating at what might lie ahead on my next trip. I didn't buy the book there and then and spent the next few days in Mallorca regretting that I hadn't. I started researching Istria online and ordered a copy of the book when I got back to the UK..

I re-evaluated the idea of driving all the way to Opatija from the UK, deciding that there was too much to see and do in Istria to waste valuable time driving there and back. It was becoming very clear that Istria would be an almost unrivalled gastronomic region and I felt it would be a great shame not to share it with someone with a high appreciation of fine food and great wines. I decided my friend Emily Glorney, a self-professed 'foodie', would be the perfect travel partner for this trip and I was delighted when she accepted the invitation to join me.

We started planning and soon realised that we couldn't see everything the area had to offer within the constraints of a week, so we had to set some priorities. Venice was a distant childhood memory for me, and Emily had never been, so we agreed we'd fly to Venice and spend the first couple of days in this unique city. This would also serve as a good context for seeing the predominantly Venetian towns along the coast of Istria.

We would drive a couple of hours to Opatija on the far eastern side of Istria for my conference. From there we would skirt our way around the Istrian coast, only 200km, taking in the deep sea 'Blue Istria'. The compact scale of the peninsula would allow for some forays inland to see the lush 'Green Istria.'

I researched some hotels and Emily ("I'm such a foodie!") came up with restaurants and some other hotel options. Our itinerary was more scheduled and pre-booked than is normal for me, but with so much to see and do we needed to be organised, making sure we would maximise the whole experience.

This book is not a guide book. There are five guides on Istria briefly reviewed at the end of this book. There is less text and more pictures than you will find in them. The pictures are placed by text that refers to these places. My aim here is more of a travelog and I am simply sharing our experience in the hope that it inspires you to visit this wonderful place. Hopefully it will help with some planning as well. You could easily spend months in Istria but its relatively small scale means a lot can be achieved in a week. I have travelled to eighty countries, and it is hard to think of a week that afforded a better travel experience than this one. My best trips abroad have been complimented by great food and wines, and, in this regard, Istria almost has no equal.

If you love the Mediterranean, but prefer it without the crowds and high prices, and are a lover of deep blue sea and amazing, lush landscapes, beautiful historic seaside towns and hilltop villages, amazing Roman ruins and great driving on empty roads, and, of course, food and wines to die for, then look no further than Istria. It's heavenly!

Cowes, England
July 2022

Venice Arrival

Unlike Istria, Venice is world renowned, and has been written about thousands of times. There are hundreds of guide books and I am not going to attempt to write another guide to this incredible city. Here, I will just retrace the steps of our wonderful two days which was a great precursor to Istria, with all its Venetian influences.

Where to Stay

Searching for hotels and restaurants online tells you right away that staying and eating in the heart of Venice is not going to be a cheap affair. There are quite a few hotels on the main island of San Marco where you can pay thousands a night. Central Venice is made up of six districts (sestieri); three on each of the two main islands divided by the famous S-shaped Grand Canal. The map looks like a hand, containing three districts grabbing the other three. San Marco, home to St Mark's Square, is the thumb of the hand. The main bridge joining the two islands is the famous Rialto Bridge, which is unmistakable the first time you see it. We stayed on the island across from San Marco as this was less hectic with tourists, a bit more residential with a local and authentic feel. And it was less expensive.

How to Arrive

The first thing you should try and stretch your finances to, is to book a private water taxi to take you into Venice from the airport. There are booths at arrivals and you can book one online for around €100. To walk out of the airport to the dock, see all the beautiful old water taxis and be whisked away at speed down the winding channel, with the iconic skyline of Venice drawing nearer on the horizon, is a truly unforgettable experience. The alternatives are one of the public water taxi boats (which we took back to the airport) or the train to the central station by the Grand Canal.

As the boat enters the inner canals joining the Grand Canal you are treated to your first views of beautiful palazzo buildings lining this main waterway. It is picturesque and you sense it's a view that is little changed from a Canaletto painting of a few hundred years ago.

We were taken to the nearest pier to our hotel (B&B Patatina) and walked across a lovely square, Campo San Giacomo da l'Orio, in the Santa Croce district. We had a room on the top floor with a small terrace balcony looking across the rooftops. It was a welcome private outside space for evening drinks and breakfast in the morning sun. We had only a couple of days in Venice, and arrived on a Sunday afternoon, knowing that many sights would be closed on Monday. But we also wanted to relax with a drink by the canal in the sun and watch the world go by on the Grand Canal. So, we did just that. Feeling suitably replenished, we walked to the Rialto Bridge and spent some time sitting on it looking down the canal. From here, we made our way to St Mark's Square via a network of narrow passageways, and with arrows pointing to 'San Marco', we made our way to St Mark's square.

My childhood memories were vague, but I recognised the distinctive domes of St Mark's Basilica down an alleyway, which signalled we were about to enter St Mark's Square. Such memories normally exaggerate the scale of things, but St Mark's Square and its 100m tall campanile were on a much grander scale than I remembered. The square is vast and the dominating campanile tower, "el paròn de casa" (the master of the house), remains the tallest structure in Venice. The tower actually collapsed in 1902 and was rebuilt by 1912.

From here, you are compelled to walk beside the Doge's Palace to the waterfront and look through mooring poles holding the rocking gondolas. You look across the Lagoon to San Giorgio Maggiore and its Palladian church and campanile that almost mirrors that of St Mark's.

The Gardens of Venice

With the tightly packed buildings separated by a labyrinth of canals and passageways, you hardly expect to see gardens in Venice. There are few large trees in the centre, but rooftops and window ledges are adorned with plants and flowers. And you get the occasional glimpse of lovely private gardens though doorways and trees over high walls and even from the canals.

Both Emily and I are keen gardeners, and each of us had recently watched Monty Don's Adriatic Gardens. I was certainly keen to see some of the gardens he'd visited in Venice. The first of these was Giardini Reali, a lovely lush public garden nestled between St Mark's Square and the Fermata boat terminal on the waterfront of the Lagoon. As it is closed on Mondays, we took the opportunity to visit while it was open on Sunday evening.

The garden was created in 1807 on Napoleon's orders, after France's conquest of the Venetian Republic. It is smaller than most city parks at just an acre (5,000 sq m) in area, but its position in the heart of Venice makes it quite something. This is a welcome green space in a city where the streets are either waterways or narrow passageways with no trees. The garden became dilapidated after WWII, and is newly restored, having only re-opened at the end of 2019. The planting is mainly lush green, repetitively structured foliage and highly scented wisteria around a central iron pergola. St Mark's campanile, rising above the royal palace, towers over the garden. It was not one of the first sights we expected to see in Venice, but we were really glad we did.

On leaving the gardens, I was curious to visit Harry's Bar just around the corner. This is where the Bellini and Carpaccio were invented. Famous visitors include Ernest Hemmingway, Charlie Chaplin, Alfred Hitchcock, Richard Burton; the list goes on and on. Unfortunately, the bar was too busy, if not a little touristy, with nowhere to sit and it also seemed sad to sit inside on this lovely sunny afternoon.

The other two gardens we saw were San Giorgio, from outside the next day, and the larger Biennale gardens the day after. I had learned from Monte Don that the Campos (squares) of Venice were originally fields and built on millions of piles. One of the big advantages of Campo San Giacomo da l'Orio, the square where we were staying, was the trees. It even had a community garden.

13

14

Taking in the atmosphere of St Mark's

One thing I remembered about St Mark's Square from my visit as a child was the orchestras playing in cafes around the square. It was just the same over four decades later. Back then, these cafes had been too expensive for us to consider on a family budget. But now I wasn't going to pass up the opportunity of sitting and watching the world go by and soaking up the atmosphere of St Mark's. A couple of drinks and some snacks at Gran Caffè Quadri cost the same as a meal in a backstreet restaurant, but sitting and relaxing in the sun with a drink in this iconic location was not to be missed.

As if by some unwritten agreement, each of the orchestras in the neighbouring cafes play a few tunes before handing the baton to next door. The music never takes a break. The square is a visual feast with fellow people-watchers seated at tables, the occasional couple dancing, people taking pictures and locals walking their dogs. You stare up and down at the majestic campanile. It looks as though it is tapered through some trick of the eye, but it isn't…or is it? The façade and domes of Saint Mark's Basilica are so intricate that you find yourself constantly discovering yet another detail that you had not previously noticed, despite an age of staring at it. The whole atmosphere washes over you.

As darkness approached on our first night, we weaved our way back through the network of alleyways and ended up dining at the Patatina restaurant right next to where were staying. The meal was delicious. Asparagus was in season and featured in several dishes. We had a starter of asparagus and prawns, and turbot with asparagus along, with some fine white wines from Veneto.

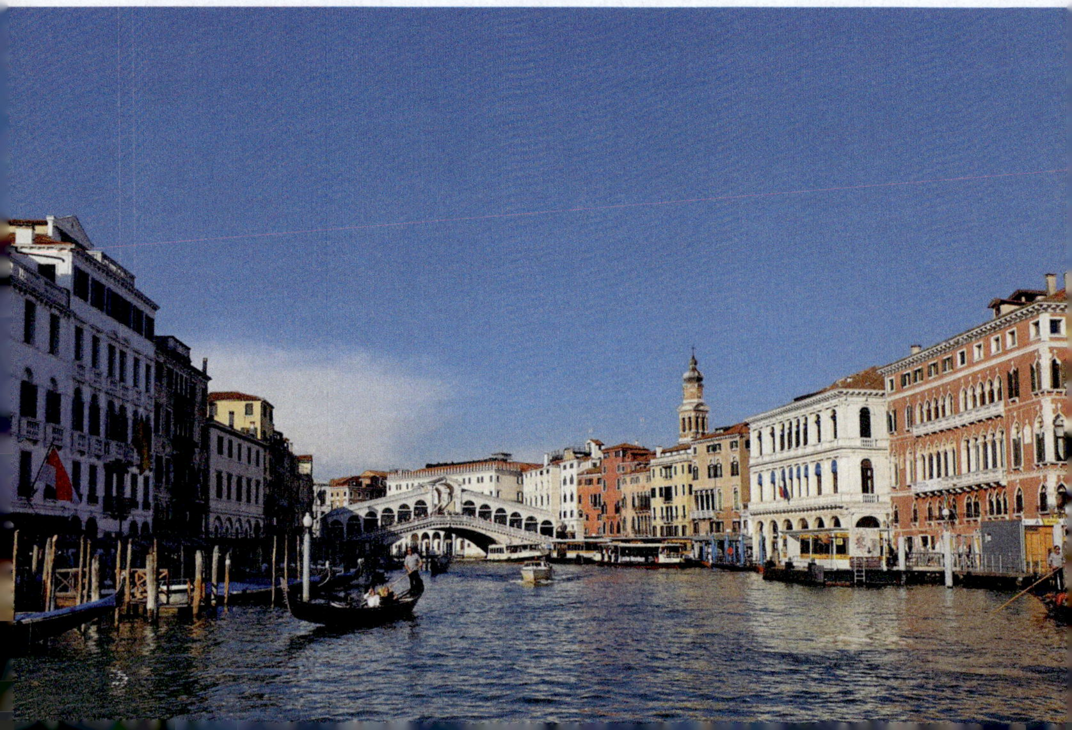

Day Two in Venice

Our first full day in Venice started with breakfast on our roof terrace looking over the roofs of Santa Croce. In fact, these wooden rooftop platforms, called altanas, are perched on roofs all over Venice as private spaces to escape the city below and catch some welcome fresh breeze. Some are decked out with lovely plants and ours was a useful vantage point for admiring several smart altanas.

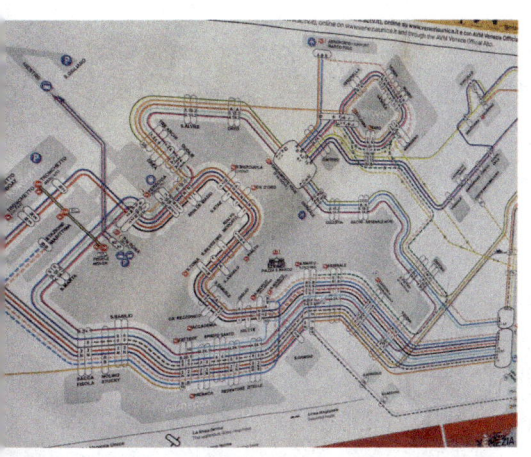

Our first challenge of the day was to navigate the labyrinth of narrow alleyways and small squares to find our nearest public ferry stop and to work out how the network of ferries operated. With no ticket office or machines at most docking piers, it turns out it is best to buy a day pass from a tobacconist. The public ferry map looks something like a metro map would in any other city, but the routes are all on the water. Our nearest stop was San Stae and we caught the boat down the Grand Canal under the Rialto Bridge to a piazza on the inner bend of the canal. We stopped here for a coffee and watched the world float by, before heading further down the canal to the Gallerie dell'Accademia, a treasure trove of Venetian painting.

An art gallery might not seem like the obvious choice for our first morning, but the magnificent grand canvases of Canaletto and Tintoretto gave us the great historic context of Venice in its heyday. The building, with its decorative ceilings, large rooms and courtyards, also gave an impression of what many of the palazzos we would drift by over two days would be like inside. It served as a reminder of Venice in its heyday, a time when rich merchants amassed vast fortunes from trading in an era where ships sucked in riches and resources from afar. Seeing the opulence of the buildings, I was reminded of Shylock in Shakespeare's 'Merchant of Venice'.

An added bonus was that the Accademia was hosting an Anish Kapor exhibition culminating with one of his signature stainless steel outdoor sculptures – a concave mirror reflecting the main courtyard. It had the wide-angle effect of bringing the more distant high walls and roofline to a closer focal point. Venice on this bright sunny day was a dramatic contrast of faded red buildings and bright blue skies. It was somehow exaggerated in this seemingly personalised mirror set before us.

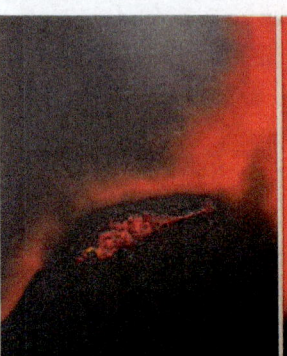

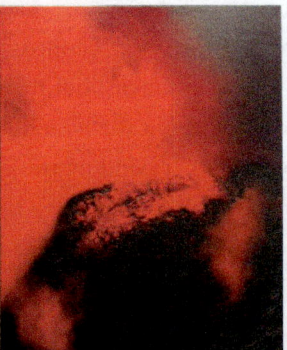

Where to eat?

On leaving the Accademia, we realised we had worked up an appetite and found a highly recommended deli, Cantine del Vino gia Schiavi, on the Rio de S. Trovaso canal nearby. The counter was covered in delicious Venetian tapas-like snacks (in fact better than tapas – sorry Spain!) with an array of wonderful combinations like prawn on asparagus paste, mushroom and truffle, sun dried tomato and mozzarella. We pretty much had two of everything with cups of white wine, and enjoyed our feast sitting on the wall by the canal in the sun.

After lunch, we walked to the end of the canal, where it met the main Venice lagoon looking across to the Island of Giudecca. It was refreshing to walk along the waterfront on the wide path with an expansive view over the water in bright sunshine, a contrast to the narrow streets and high buildings elsewhere. . We walked all the way to the point of the Dorsodouro district and went inside the Basilica di Santa Maria della Salute. There are many grand churches dotted around Venice and the grey domes of this district mark the skyline when you look right from the waterfront at St Mark's.

San Giorgio Maggiore

We caught the boat across the mouth of the Grand Canal where it meets the lagoon back to St Mark's. As we walked past the Doge's Palace and the Bridge of Sighs to the San Zaccaria boat terminal, the waterfront was much more crowded. From here, we crossed the lagoon to the enticing island of San Giorgio Maggiore. We had the spacious paved waterfront to ourselves and sat on the slabs looking back across the lagoon to the iconic skyline of St Mark's.

We would have like to have seen the gardens of the Giorgio Cini Foundation, but they were closed on Mondays. We did, however, manage to walk around and see the immaculate Borges Labyrinth in the back of the gardens. As mazes go, it is hard to think of one that could beat this. It is made up of a kilometre of paths and over 3,000 box plants around two meters high. It was planted only a decade ago and inspired by the works of the Argentinian writer Jorge Luis Borges, who was in love with the natural labyrinth of streets and canals of Venice, its history and complexity. Perhaps the most unique feature of the labyrinth is, that when it is seen from above, it reflects the shape of an open book that spells out his name. So, see it from high above we would do.

The highlight of this trip across the water was going to the top of Campanile di San Giorgio. The top of the St Mark's Campanile is the more obvious choice, but there was a big queue, it cost more and the view would be one of looking directly down on the

heart of Venice below. The tower on the small island at San Giorgio gives a better perspective, I think, of St Mark's and the surrounding archipelago. The views are spectacular and you are not fighting a crowd of people to enjoy them. We spent about an hour up there taking in the amazing vista. Going to the top of San Giorgio Maggiore is definitely one of my top recommendations for Venice.

We took the boat back to San Zaccaria and walked along to St Mark's Square and returned to Quadri (yes, it's that good) for drinks while taking in the atmosphere. We were there earlier in the afternoon than the day before and it was good to sit in the hot bright sun and view the more brightly lit façade of St Mark's Basilica.

San Zaccaria boat station is one stop before the main St Mark's stop, and not too far, so we walked back there to get the boat home. Doing so set us up brilliantly for getting front seats on the boat ride all the way home, watching the whole of the Grand Canal unfold before us. A trip to Venice would be incomplete without this ride down the length of the Grand Canal.

We watched the boat fill up and empty again as we went from nearly the start to the end of this line in a way that a tube might from start to finish on the London Underground. Having navigated the full S of the Grand Canal, we got off at the Riva de Biasio stop and walked to Canal Grand Hotel, the site of our first drink in Venice the day before. Here we sat at the water's edge looking across the canal to the central railway station bathing in the setting sun,, and the comings and goings of early evening on the water. We noticed a secret canal-side rose garden in the super smart Ca'Nigra Lagoon Resort and thought we would have our next drink there. As we waited to be served, the fading warmth of the sun, mosquitos and a growing hunger for dinner got the better of us and we left.

Near here was a simple small eatery that was highly recommended through online reviews. We had tried to get a table the night before and again on this evening there was a queue waiting for the next table to come free. We decided that our appetites could not last the distance so we went on a hunt and ended up at another lovely restaurant, Il Refolo, with tables set right on a paved area by a little bridge over a small canal. We were just on the other side of our square and returned to our private roof terrace for a bottle of red watching the surrounding rooftops grow into silhouettes as the evening grew darker.

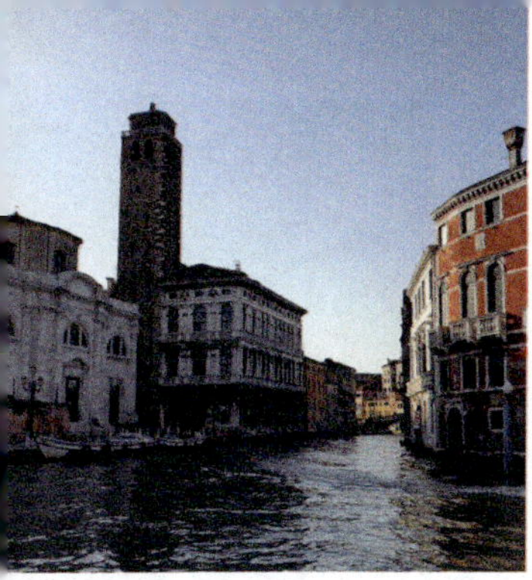
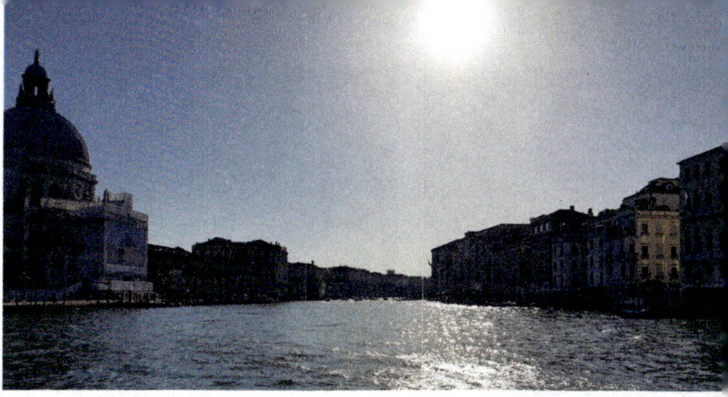
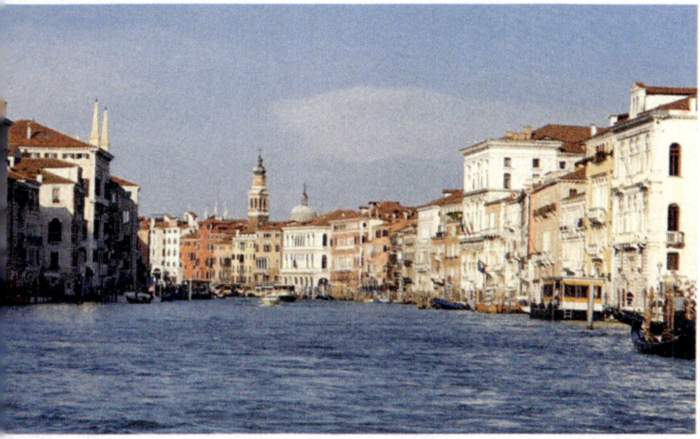
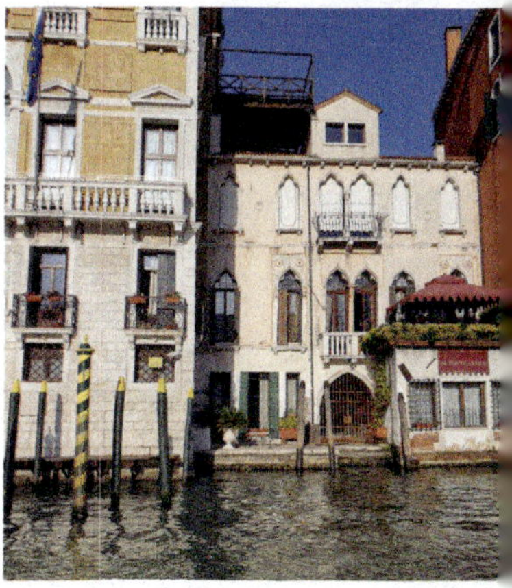
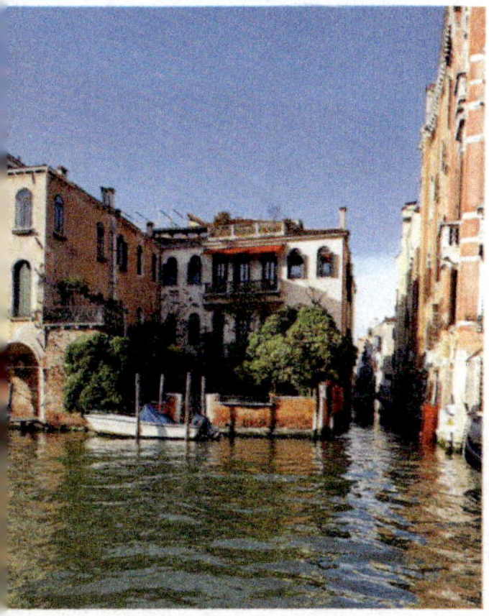
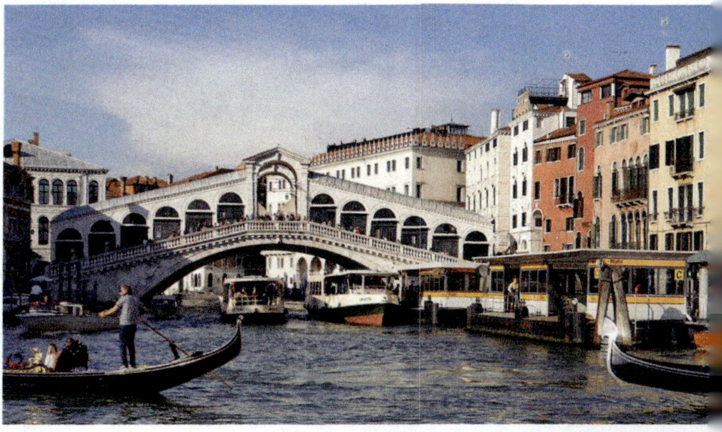
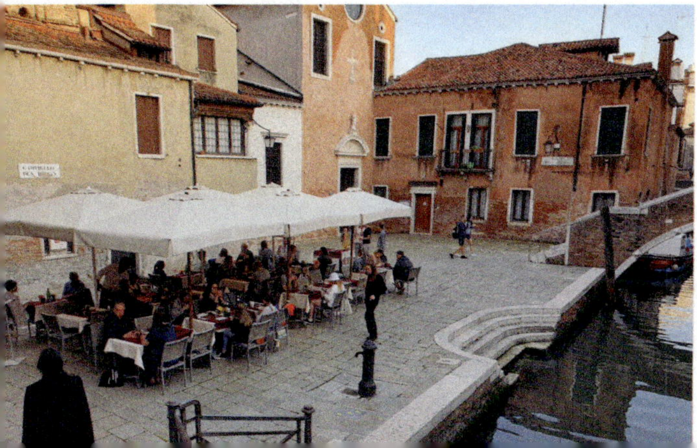
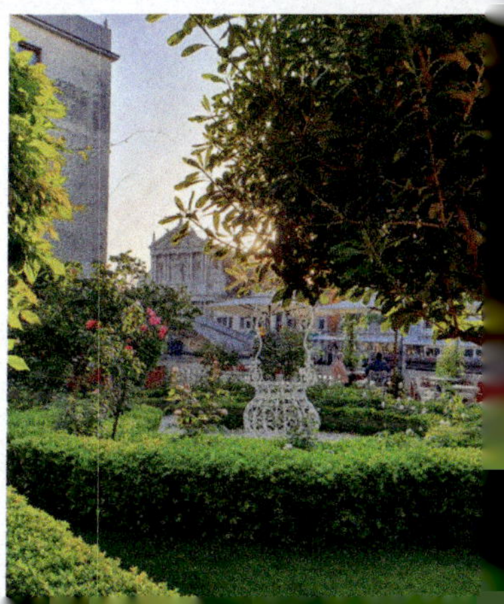

24

Our last day in Venice

Today we would be leaving Venice for Istria around lunch time. We had decided the evening before that we just had to see the Venice Biennale. The world's largest art fair is held in Venice every second summer and we both felt we would be mad to miss it. We had come to appreciate that the quickest way to get anywhere in Venice was on foot. Instead of snaking down the Grand Canal and stopping at every boat stop, we could take a more direct route through the labyrinth of alleyways and squares to get to where we needed at our own pace. It also afforded us the opportunity to stop wherever we wanted.

The first such stop was the Rialto Fish Market, where the fresh fish from the Adriatic is brought up the canal and unloaded. It was visually stunning and an interesting start to the day. We had a morning coffee again at one of the cafes on the Campo Erbiria.

There are few modern buildings in Venice and as a result there are lots of small shops in the passageways, with artisan offerings. We found a great shop selling beautiful stationary, ink quills and wax seals. The glassware is world-renowned. Venice is also world famous for its annual festival, where period costumes and elaborate masks are worn, and many a shop window is adorned with an array of masks. We visited one shop where they were making the masks from papier mâché, and painting them with intricate and highly decorative pattens. You are unlikely to ever find such a selection of amazing masks anywhere else in the world. They just had to be tried on.

We made our way to St Mark's Square, turning left at the waterfront and walking all the way along the side of the lagoon until we reached the entrance of the Venice Biennale. This international cultural exhibition is held in The Arsenal in the Castello district, the largest of Venice's sestieri. The venue is perfect for the event and is almost as impressive as the art on show. The Arsenal is a complex of shipyards and former armouries. It was responsible for the bulk of the Venetian Republic's naval power. Construction began in the twelfth century and by the height of the powers of the republic it had become the largest industrial complex in Europe, only to be finally conquered by Napoleon in 1797. This area is more spread out than the heart of Venice, and wandering around these old dockyards was a refreshing change to the touristy centre.

Venice Biennale

The Biennale cleverly leads you though a succession of old warehouses. The contrast of this historic backdrop and modern art works brilliantly. It was a sensory overload and we lost ourselves for the few hours meandering through the vast exhibition. I left feeling quite overwhelmed and a walk through the Giardini della Biennale, the only real park in Venice, was a welcome come down. Whether you are a fan of modern art or not, if you find yourself in Venice while it is on, it is well worth experiencing.

We walked back to the centre through some of the back streets, which gave us a flavour of residential Venetian life. We even saw a group of locals in costumes and masks on their way to a wedding. We walked through St Mark's Square one last time, and then, when we got back to our neighbourhood at lunchtime, made one last attempt to dine at the small eatery we had tried a few times. Success! Bacaro Quebrado is a simple taverna. We were initially drawn to it by the outstanding online reviews.

The menu was highly original and I always love to try new food combinations. The highlight was their signature 'saor' dishes. We chose the one with fresh large prawns – scampi. These are shelled and lightly dusted with un-toasted breadcrumbs and then mixed in what can be best described as sauerkraut, though the taste was more subtle. The dish looks a little like a seafood pasta, but tastes very different, with a sweet and sour flavour. It tricks you. It's a sort of seafood salad with Germanic roots. I am tempted to have a go at making it myself.

The menu stated: 'The saor is a typical dish of the maritime tradition of the lagoon, dating back to 1300 when, given the need of sailors and fishermen to preserve the fish as long as possible, it was designed as this "sauce". The fish was placed in a bowl and, between one layer and another, one of onions cooked in a pan over a low heat with the addition of wine vinegar and sometimes white wine, raisins and pine nuts. Historically, the addition of onion was linked to the aggression and elimination of bacteria that, in the absence of coolers, led to the deterioration of food.'

Time was passing us by and we needed to get to the airport to pick up our hire car to drive to Croatia. We decided to take the ferry to the airport. The only real option for buying public transport tickets in Venice is via the network of tobacconists. They all close for lunch, and it seems they all open later than the signs stating their hours of business indicate. Domani, domani. We subsequently missed our boat and waited an hour in our local square. There are worse places to sit.

As the fast ferry weaved along the windy canal to the airport, we watched the skyline of Venezia grow smaller. It had been an amazing couple of days. If you have never been to Venice, you absolutely must go. If you have been, you don't need me to tell you that. Venice is like nowhere else in the world and you'll want to go again.

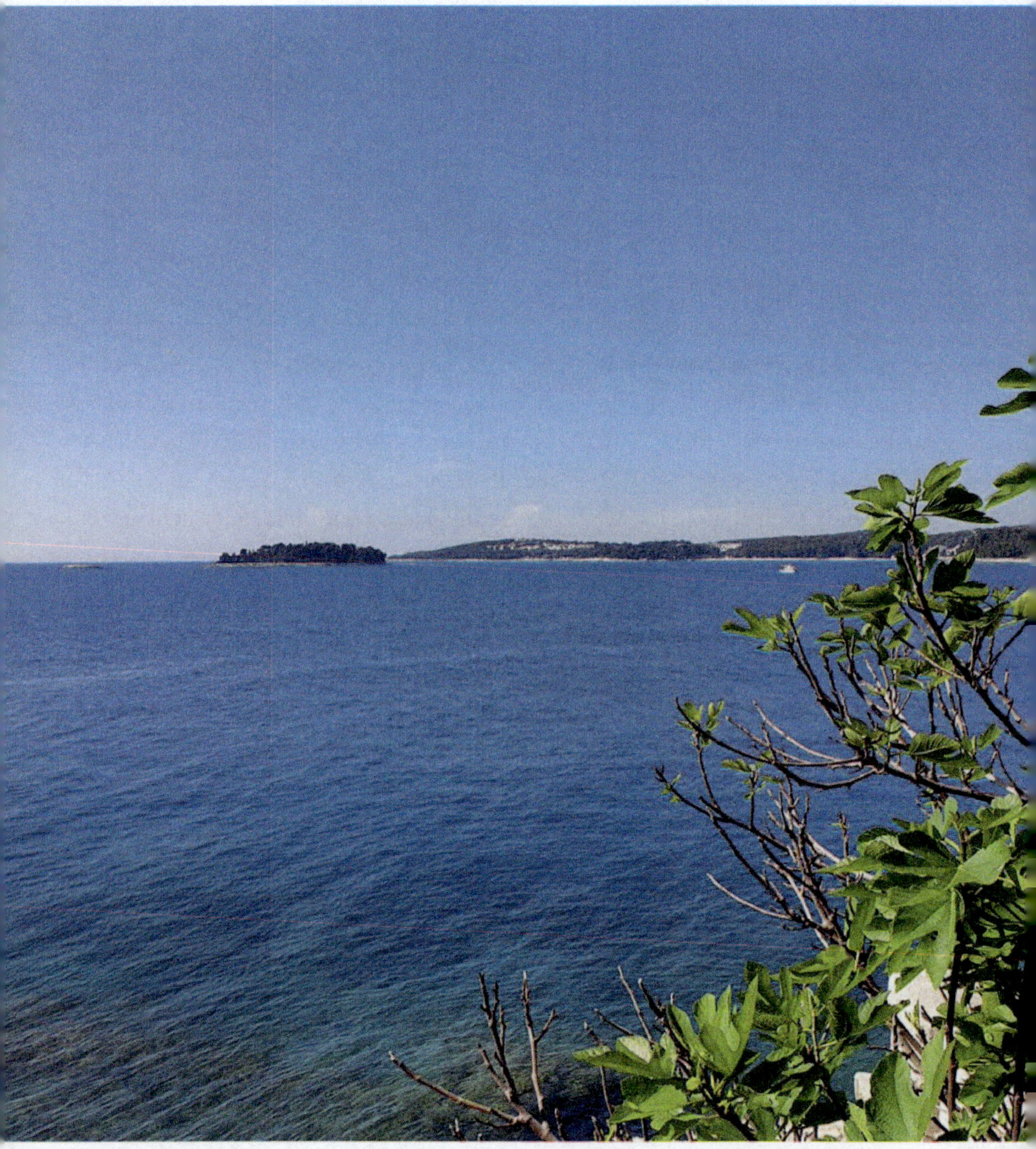

ISTRIA

About Istria

Istria is a heart-shaped peninsula pointing southwards at the very northern end of the Adriatic Sea. It is around 70km across at the top and 100km long from the north to the southern point. The region is almost entirely in Croatia, but takes in a small part of Slovenia – and its only coastline, of 40km – on the western side. In fact, the shortest distance coast to coast across the top of the peninsula also takes in a tiny slither of Italy below Trieste. While Istria doesn't really take in a meaningful part of Italy, the Italian influence is so strong that it feels very Italian in much of the region. Istria must be one of Europe's best kept secrets. It is packed with centuries of history and wonderful scenery and is a complete gastronomic experience with amazing local food and wines. The renowned Michelin Guide in 2018 listed an incredible fifteen Istrian restaurants, with eight of these concentrated in the north west of the province around Novigrad.

History

Istria takes its name from the Histri tribe, which inhabited the region from around 1,000 BC. The Romans conquered Istria in 177 BC near Pula, where the magnificent amphitheatre still stands, and Istria became an important source of olive oil and wine. Following the collapse of the Roman Empire in AD 476, Byzantium established control in the 6th century. The Euphrasius Basilica at Porec, now a UNESCO World Heritage Site, was built during this time. The Slavs and the Lombards followed until Istria was annexed by the Frankish ruler Charlemagne in AD789.

Venetian rule of Istria was fully established in 1267 after a few hundred years of controlling most of the west coast of the peninsula. Outbreaks of plague in the 17th century devastated the population of Istria, reducing the number of inhabitants at Pula to a mere few hundred people. The Venetian Republic ended with the arrival of Napoleon in 1797 but when Napoleon met his Waterloo in 1815, the Austrian Hapsburg empire took control. The Germanic influence is clearly visible in the spa town of Opatija.

After World War I, Istria was given to Italy by treaty and in the 1920s the rise of Italian fascism took hold, leading to one of first anti-fascist groups in Europe being born. During World War II, Istria was effectively occupied by the Nazis via the Italian alliance. With the end of the war in 1945, Croatia, including Istria, became part of Tito's communist Yugoslavia. This led to an exodus of some 300,000 Italians fearing reprisals. Croatian independence was established in 1991 and the country became part of the EU in 2013.

Getting There and Getting Around

We hired a car at Venice airport and drove just over two hours to Opatija on the far side of Istria. But there are rail, air, water and other road options.

Air: EasyJet and Ryanair fly to Pula from London. There are also low-cost flights direct to Pula from Birmingham and Manchester in the summer, as well as from other European airports. Other nearby airports include Rijeka, close to Opatija, Trieste, Ljubljana and Zagreb.

Rail: There are train services to Rijeka, Pula from Zagreb and Koper in Slovenia from Ljubljana, but realistically this is not the best way to get to and around Istria because there is so much to see and experience between these transport hubs.
Road: There are buses to Istria and around the coast of the peninsula which might be a good option for budget travellers and it would also make a great cycling holiday given the relatively short distances and quiet roads. In fact, there are established and signposted road cycling routes around Istria, with accessible DIY mechanical support stations at designated intervals along the way.

Water: There are ferries from Trieste and Venice to Porec, Rovinj, Pula and Piran which make a day trip to Venice viable or a short visit to each of these lovely Istrian towns possible from Italy.

Cycling: We saw quite a lot of people on bicycles, ranging from racers to people clearly taking their time. Touring route signs and facilities were visible along the way.

Istria is predominantly a rural region so perhaps the most practical way to see it is by car. However, if you rent outside of Croatia, ensure that your hire car company permits cross-national travel. I searched for companies hiring in Italy and dropping off at the airport in Zagreb, and then checked the small print on available options.

I hired from Alamo, which turned out to be Locauto. We had a great hybrid Fiat 500. I didn't take out full insurance as I have an annual worldwide hire car insurance policy which is much more cost effective. Locauto said scratches on the car up to 5cm were fine but when we returned the car, they pointed to scratches on the wheel rims (apparently not part of the car) and charged me an extra €240. Welcome to Italy!

The Colours of Istria

I picked up a pamphlet describing the colours of Istria, which I felt embodied this visually stunning region. All the guide books talk of Blue Istria, by the sea, and Green Istria, inland, but this included a few more and here is a precis:

Blue Istria – emphasises the difference between coastal communities and inland. For centuries people looked primarily to the sea and Venice as the economic and cultural power. The coast provided prosperity with ports for fishing, salt, textiles, tobacco, spices and rock aggregates under the Venetian Republic.

Green Istria – depicts the lush inland landscape of densely wooded hills, providing a profusion of shades of green as far as the eye can see. The annual spring foraging for wild asparagus found all over the region embodies Green Istria. The contrast between the lush green woodland and the deep blue sea is greater than anywhere I can think of.

Red Istria – represents the rich deep red volcanic soil, terra rossa, which is mostly responsible for the outstanding produce of the region. Compacted with little humus, it soaks up water easily and holds it for a long time, allowing plants to survive long dry and hot summers. This combined with the Mediterranean climate makes the soil ideal for cultivating grapes and olives.

Grey Istria – is for the hilly lands of central Istria, particularly around Pazin where barren slopes can be seen. This is also reflected in the stone of the medieval buildings of the hilltop towns and villages found inland.

White Istria – refers to the mountain ranges in the northernmost part of the peninsula. This hilly limestone landscape is particularly suitable for sheep farming.

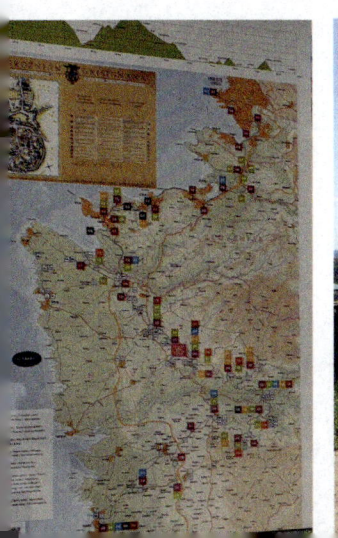

36

Opatija

Our Drive to Istria

With our delays getting out of Venice, we ended up driving to Opatija into the early evening. The drive from Venice to Trieste on the autostrada is relatively flat and then rises up into more mountainous territory. Soon after, you cross the border seamlessly into Slovenia. Starting our tour of the region in the top eastern corner of Istria meant we would drive the coast from the furthest eastern point working our way back around the coast and, as it materialised, with the most exciting towns to follow.

Our route from Trieste to Opatija took us 50km across the top of Istria through the Capodistria region. Almost as soon as we crossed the border into Slovenia, the countryside softened to a more rural and lush tranquil landscape. We stopped at passport control at the Slovenia-Croatia border, where the scenery changed again with the more dramatic barren mountains of the Kvarner Region to the north east. From here we drove 20km to Opatija at top of the eastern Istrian coast. The Uckar and Cicarija mountains rise 1,400m above this seaside spa resort so the final descent into town is quite dramatic.

Opatija was the whole reason for this trip in the first place. I was speaking at a conference at the Grand Hotel Adriatic the following morning. My accommodation search showed the resort was full of large hotels and I felt that this would not be a highlight of Istria. I expected to be disappointed, but as we drove the winding terraced roads down into town at nightfall, we were pleasantly surprised.

Opatija is like a Germanic version of Monaco. The town developed into an extremely fashionable resort for the well-heeled elite during Austrian rule. It became the perfect seaside playground just a few hours south for landlocked Europeans. When I was looking at places to stay, I chose the Savoy Hotel. This was one of the few waterfront hotels and I sensed that it might have a bit of a faded charm. The other glitzier hotels had the main road running in front of them, though it turned out the road was quiet. We parked right outside the hotel front door (the benefit and charm of the Fiat 500) and were told we could leave the car there. I was already liking this place. From our balcony we looked over the peaceful Adriatic. This seemed a far cry from the crowds of Venice and we relaxed surveying the view with a drink.

Emily had booked us into Bevanda, the best restaurant in town, but we had arrived late and didn't want to rush so we switched our reservation to the following night. Instead, we chose a table on the terrace at the restaurant (Lungomare) attached to the hotel. This seemingly less inspiring hotel restaurant was to be our first Istrian food experience.

Our first taste of Istria

In writing about Istria, I considered producing a section devoted to the amazing food and wines. But I decided it was best to share the gastronomic journey as we progressively found it. This fairly typical restaurant on our first night eased us in gently without the taste explosion that fine dining would entail.

Our starting point was the wine list and we discussed the options with the helpful waiter, Hrvoje, who brought wines to the table for us to try. Istria's signature white grape is Malvazija, so this was our natural starting point. There are over eighty vineyards in this small pocket of Europe and there were lots to choose from on the menu. The Malvazija grape originates from Greece and is grown in other places around the Mediterranean, the Canaries and even California, but Istria provides the perfect combination of growing elements. The wine is a crisp, dry, medium bodied wine. The nearest wine I could think it tasted like is an Austrian Gruner Veltliner, though less fruity. The nose was one of grapefruit for me and the finish was ever so slightly of bitter herbs. The minerality really shone through and this mouth-watering white became our 'go to' wine for the rest of the trip.

We ordered a fresh scampi risotto to share and tuna steaks for mains, but the next taste sensation after the wine was what came with the bread. An unlabelled bottle of local olive oil was placed on the table and the waiter lingered to see our reaction. Istrian olive oil is so good you feel you could drink it. The flavour is slightly stronger and more peppery than the mass produced extra virgin olive oil we have grown used to buying in the UK. It is a bit greener in colour, with fruity overtones. Istria has a history of producing olive oil since Roman times. Because the region is small, it is mostly organically grown by small-batch producers and is of excellent quality, rarely exported to the UK.

And then, to top all this off, the scampi risotto arrived. The combination of the bread and olive oil, the rich risotto and the crisp local wine in this simple restaurant in the heat of the night with a slight sea breeze was heavenly. Before our mains arrived, it was time to talk red wines with our waiter. Istria's red grape is Teran and we went with his recommendation. In fact, Hrvoje told us confidently, "if you don't like it, we will drink it." It was a big red, in more ways than one, arriving in a one-litre bottle which I thought was inspired. After a lifetime of feeling that 750cl was not quite enough, here was such an obvious solution to the problem. Why have we restricted ourselves to 750cl bottles all these years?

The Teran grape is uniquely suited to the Istrian climate. It is late ripening and grows in large clusters of densely packed berries. The vine requires a lot of sun, but not scorching hot as that would burn the grapes. Low rainfall is fine, but excessive humidity is especially problematic with the risk of botrytis fungal attack. The western shores of Istria are perfect for cultivating the Teran grape and consequently it is the predominant red wine of the region.

When the first glass was poured for us to taste, it was a deep ruby red, almost purple. The colour tricked me into thinking this would be a big full-bodied red like a cabernet sauvignon, full of tannins, but it was much softer than its appearance suggested. Again, the minerality showed through and the fruity aroma was quite addictive. This paired perfectly with our delicious tuna steaks.

Other grapes, such as merlot, chardonnay, pinot grigio and cabernet sauvignon, are grown in the region, but the Malvazija and the Teran were so new and exciting to us that we barely deviated from these two varieties for the rest of the trip. Having expected a relatively unexciting late dinner, our first meal in Istria turned out to be a sign of things to come.

The next morning, I went straight to the conference I was speaking at. Emily went for a run along the stunning seafront promenade track that runs for 12km along the coast of the Kvarner Bay, with pockets of small beaches – designated separately for humans and dogs – rocky coastline, and highly scented foliage. I walked back from the conference along a small section of the track and rather regretted that I didn't have time to explore it further. The promenade is known as the Lungomare, our restaurant namesake from the previous night. The afternoon was spent by the hotel pool on the waterfront and a swim in the crystal-clear sea was called for.

For our second night in Opatija, dinner was at Bevanda. We walked along the promenade through soft scented sea front gardens to the park in front of Villa Amalia. Bevanda is a stunning modern building set on a promontory by a little port next to the yacht club on the Lungomare. The plate glass restaurant windows allow for views across the sea towards the larger resort of Rijeka and the islands. We were treated to an amazing crimson sky at sunset. The sea was so calm that it took on a thickly viscous oil-like appearance.

The food at Bevanda was incredible, and fresh fish dishes and fine wines flowed. Raw tuna with a crunchy truffle dust on the side followed by turbot with a light pistachio crust. If you go to Opatija, this is definitely the place to eat!

We wouldn't have chosen to stay two nights in Opatija, but our late arrival on the first night and the conference meant it was more practical to do so. I expected to be unimpressed with the town but was pleasantly surprised. If you are spending a week in Istria, spare a night for Opatija. The coast here is very different from the rest of Istria and the town's Austrian-Hungarian historical influences make it an interesting contrast to the visible Italian influence on the Western and Southern coasts.

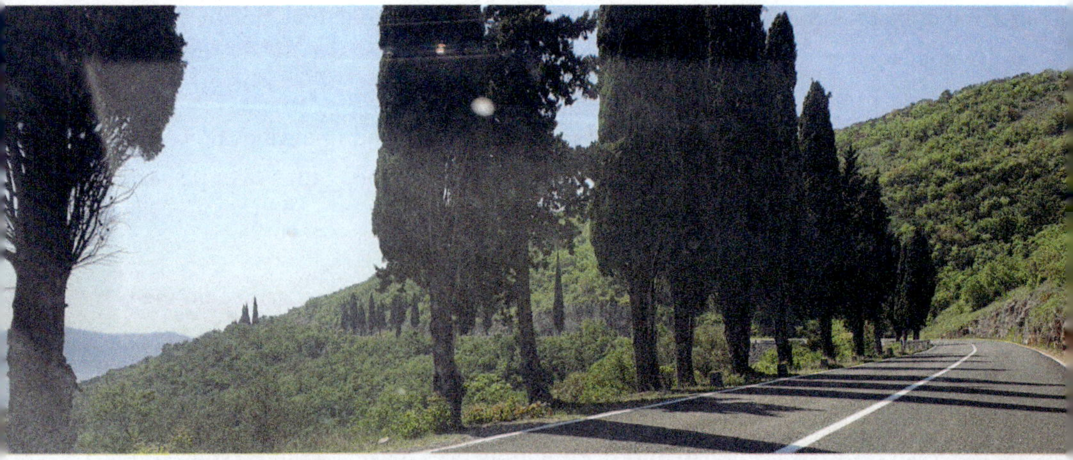

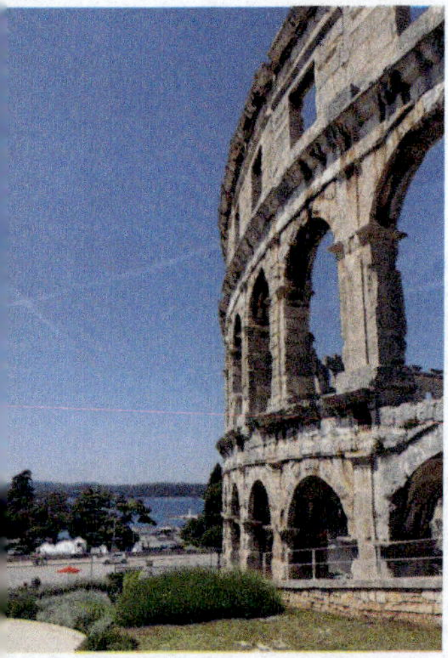

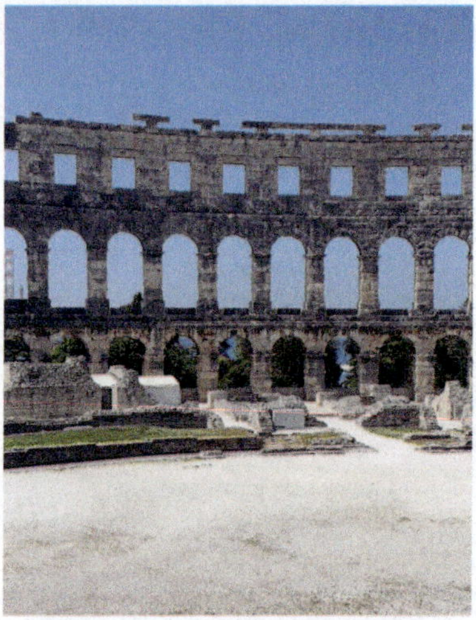

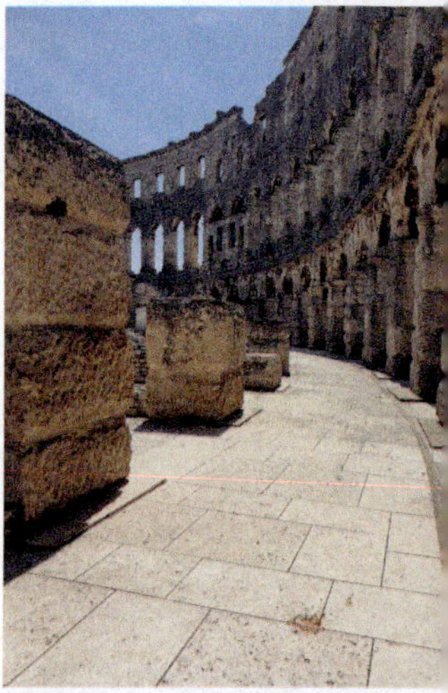

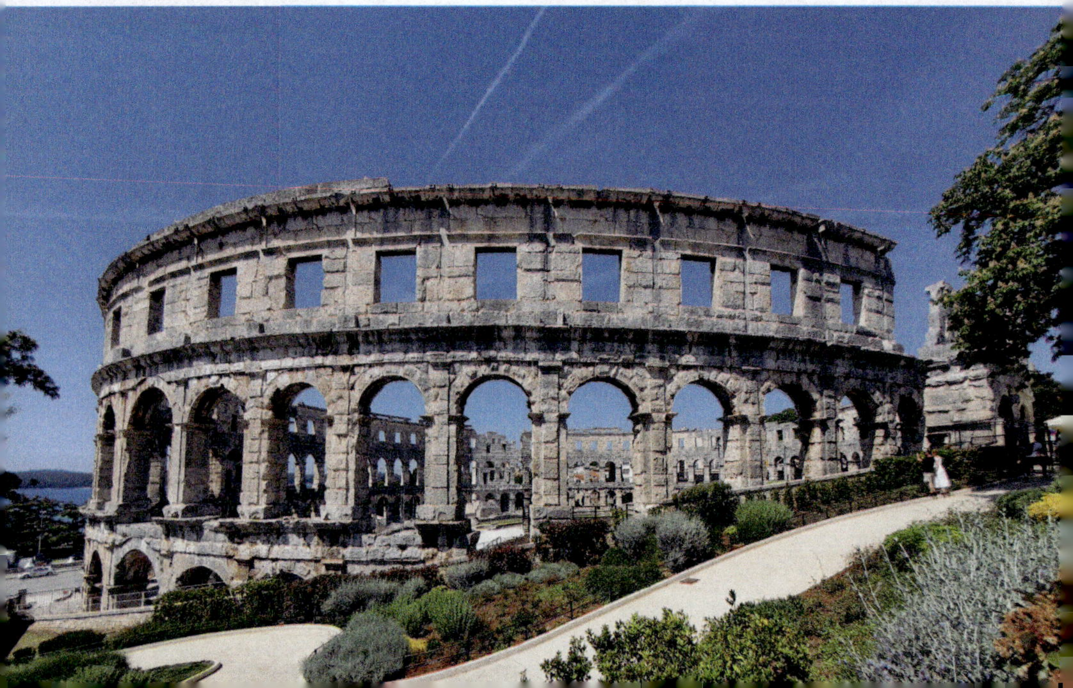

Pula

Driving down the East Coast

Perhaps one of the biggest advantages of choosing Opatija as a starting point for a drive around the coast of Istria is the stunning drive south along the east coast. This is 'Blue Istria' at its very best. The coast is mountainous on this side of the peninsula and as you wind your way along the tree-lined coastal roads you are constantly afforded views across the deep blue sea out to the islands of north Croatia – hence 'Blue Istria', as it is known by the locals.

Our lunchtime destination was Pula, Istria's largest town. The 85km drive from Opatija took 90 minutes and the major purpose of our visit was to see the Roman amphitheatre. This spectacular arena with circular arched walls is reminiscent of the colosseum in Rome and rivals the arenas in Nimes and Arles in the South of France. We had the place to ourselves, and as we stood in the middle of the stadium could easily imagine roaring crowds and lions bounding out of the tunnels towards us. In its time, the amphitheatre held a capacity crowd of 20,000 people. You can feel the history. There is a museum in the tunnels below … where the lions and less fortunate would have been held. The museum was well presented, with glimpses of Roman life and a useful, brief, history of the context of the amphitheatre.

We walked around the external perimeter of the amphitheatre, part of a public gardens, then down to the harbour. We had made the most of the Opatija hotel breakfast that morning, which included planning ahead for a makeshift lunch. So, we sat in the park down by the harbour and enjoyed a free lunch not far from the innocent smile of our Fiat 500. We had a quick wander around Pula, but we were keen to make our way to the north west along 40km of coastline to Rovinj.

44

Rovinj

If there is one iconic Venetian town in Istria, it is Rovinj. Rovinj was originally an island, but in 1763 the Habsburgs filled in the sea between the island and the isthmus, turning it into the small peninsula it is today. I felt this would be the absolute 'must see' of this trip and I wasn't disappointed. I booked the best hotel I could find. Hotel Angelo D'Oro is a 17th century former bishop's palace half way up the hill that is the top of Rovinj. There are no cars in the town and we drove to a satellite hotel car park where the hotel staff came and picked us up in an electric buggy. As we approached the town and turned up the narrow-cobbled street to the hotel, I was almost pinching myself at the magical beauty of this place.

Rovinj is unmistakably Venetian. Rovinj gives one an impression of the power of the Venetian Empire. Seeing Venice gives Rovinj a useful context and vice versa. The campanile that dominates the town is almost a carbon copy of St Mark's in Venice. The brightly coloured houses of Venetian reds and ochres around the edge of the town meet the water just as they would on the Grand Canal. Much of the stone used to construct Venice was transported across the sea from here. There are boat services from Venice that take a few hours, but to only do a day trip and miss the sunset and sunrise when the colours take on a different hue would be a real shame.

The Angelo D'Oro is a lovely 4-star boutique hotel and our room had a wonderful view through the buildings out to sea. It was late afternoon and we were keen to explore the town. We turned left out of the hotel door and walked up the street to a park surrounding the baroque catholic Church of Saint Euphemia that crowns Rovinj. There are commanding views across the sea and we spent an hour taking in the church and its breathtaking surroundings. There is no doubting the Italian influence of the place.

Leaving the church, we walked further around the end of the peninsula dropping back down to sea level where we had an afternoon drink at the lovely waterfront restaurant bar, La Puntulina. They were setting up the tables for dinner right on the rocks looking out to sea and a small part of me thought this would be a great place for dinner, but Emily had already reserved the top restaurant in town as her treat to me and it looked like La Puntulina was fully booked.

We walked around the rest of the atmospheric back streets and alleyways, reaching the main harbour before heading back to the hotel to change for dinner. We had twenty minutes to kill before our restaurant booking and returned to La Puntulina for sundowners. It really is the place to be at sunset in Rovinj.

47

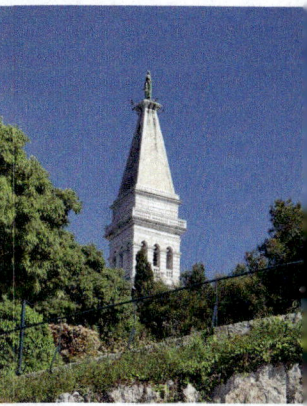

Dinner at Monte

Emily had already done the research and for her Monte was the only option in Rovinj. This is Croatia's first restaurant to be awarded a Michelin star. The restaurant is at the top of town, just under the ramparts of the church and feels very intimate with no more than 20 diners. There are three tasting menus (6 courses + intro and finale) and you can put together your own selection from each of them. There were two classic Istrian menus; one more traditional and one focusing on the rawness and providence

of the local food. The third menu offering new and exciting taste combinations is what we went for. And, of course there was the wine pairing with each course, which, for us, felt obligatory. We had an absolutely stunning meal and while not cheap by Istrian standards, it probably comes at a price below most Michelin-starred restaurants elsewhere. If you go to Rovinj and can afford to push the boat out, this is a wonderful experience. We had amazing food everywhere in Istria, but this meal came top. Thank you, Emily!

I woke early the next morning and decided to get up and catch Rovinj at sunrise. The colours reflecting in the water slowly brought the town alive and afforded me the cover picture of this book. Emily went to the morning market where she found local produce including olive oil and truffles. We had a long slow breakfast in the lovely hotel garden and as we were checking out, they presented us with a bottle of their 'house' olive oil.

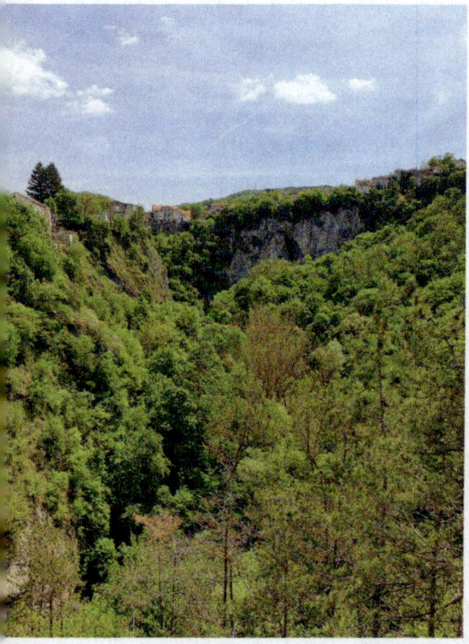

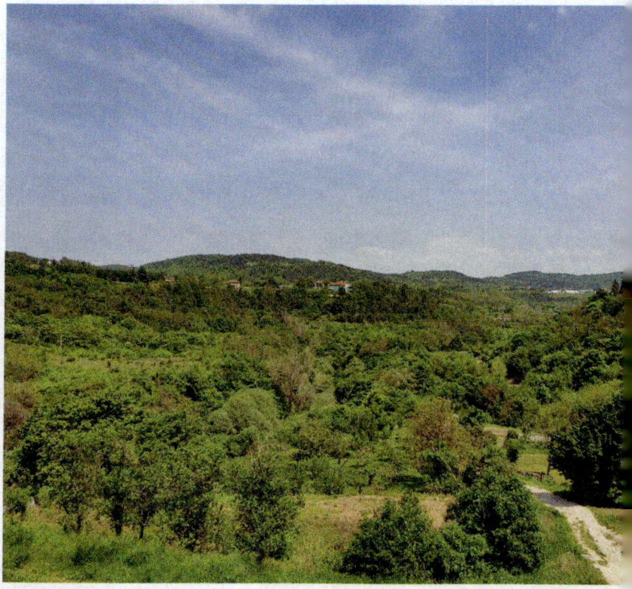

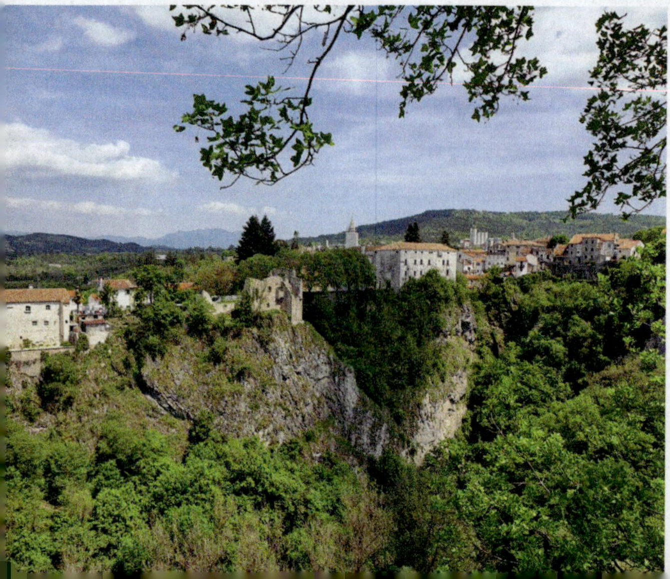

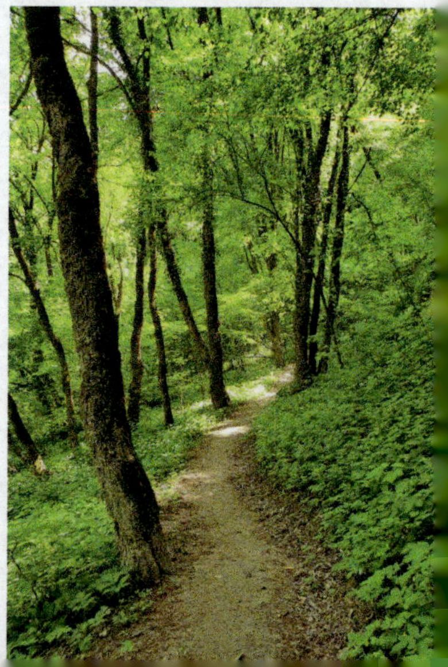

Pazin

Istria's small scale allows for short trips into the interior. Our next night was to be in Poreč. While only 20km up the coast as the crow flies, the Limski Kanal penetrates several kilometres inland which doubles the driving distance. We had already decided to drive on the extra 20 minutes to Pazin, the capital located in the dead centre of the Istrian peninsula.

Inland, Istria's karst geography becomes really clear. The gradual action of relatively acidic rainwater slowly dissolves limestone to create a profusion of caves and sinkholes. This landscape is most apparent in the medieval town of Pazin, with its castle set on the edge of a gorge. The castle, set on four enclosed floors around a central courtyard, contained a museum with some interesting displays of history, including some photos of the communist invasion post WWII.

From the castle we walked down the winding path to the floor of the gorge. It was a lovely walk in the shaded woods. The cliff below the castle falls 100m to the 'Pazin abyss', a cave and sinkhole, at its base. This is famed for the dramatic escape of the hero Mathius Sandorf in the eponymous Jules Verne novel, and is also thought to have provided the inspiration for the entrance to Hell in Dante's Inferno. There is a sign on the trail detailing expeditions of explorers who discovered underground lakes via a vast network of underground tunnels and chambers.

As we were nearing the end of our walk, we entered a sunny clearing where we chanced upon a 6ft green snake. It slowly slithered away as we froze in our tracks. From then on, I kept seeing snakes for the rest of the walk.

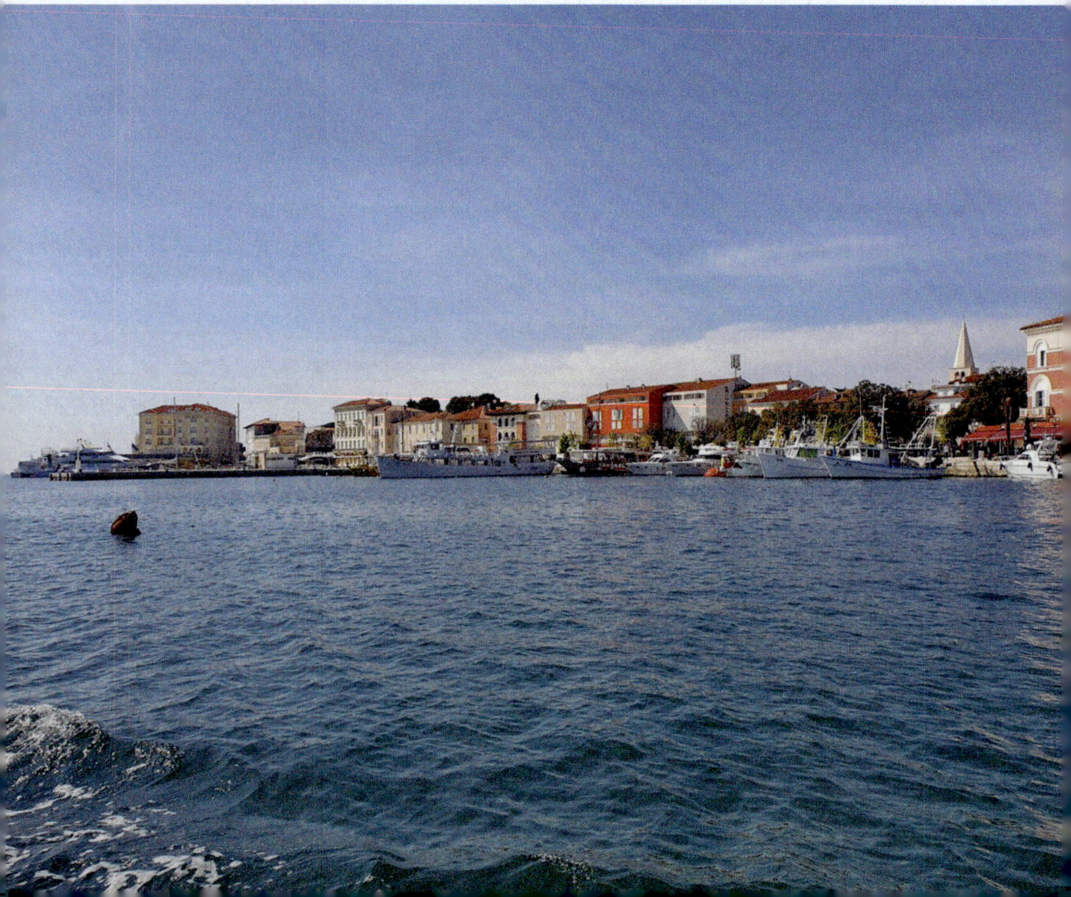

Poreč

In Roman times, Poreč was the capital of Istria. It is bigger and flatter than Rovinj, with much more accommodation and therefore tourists staying overnight. The first thing I noticed when we arrived was how much more widely Italian was spoken; there are boats to Poreč from Venice. We booked an apartment for one night, which was managed by the Valamar Resort Group who had a few locations here. An advantage of this was that we were able to use the locations across the Group network and as it was a hot afternoon, we caught the hotel water taxi over to the Isabella resort on the small Sveti Nikola Island, a few hundred metres away. Here we could relax with drinks by the pool and beach sunlounges and cool off on this hot afternoon with swims in the sea. It was a very different experience from Rovinj, but it was a good option for chilling that afternoon and the free ferry crossing afforded views of the mainland that offered a perspective of Poreč from the water.

We headed back to our apartment on Trg Matije Gupca, a large open square which also contains the well-preserved Romanesque House. This was unfortunately closed: it usually is, apparently. Poreč is very clearly Roman. The main street, Decumanus, runs the several hundred metre length of the peninsula. Perpendicular to this is Cardo Maximus. We wandered around the town that night to get our bearings for exploring it properly the next morning and ewre struck by a more buzzy nightlife than in previous places we had visited in Istria.

We had determined to have dinner at one of the konobas that evening. These taverns or cellars are the soul of Croatian rustic cuisine, akin to a tapas bar in Spain. It also made a nice contrast from our high-end dining of the night before. Konoba Aba down an alleyway off the Decumanus was our choice. We sat at a table outside in the alleyway. The food and service were great, especially considering that the owner's large family had returned from all over Europe for a wedding. We started with truffle pasta followed by an amazing seafood platter. After dinner we walked around the fairly deserted streets of the town.

Our major mission the next morning was to visit the Euphrasian Basilica, Poreč's main attraction. Built in the 6th century, the site was ascribed to the UNESCO World Heritage list in 1997. The beautiful mosaics constitute one of the finest examples of early Byzantine architecture to be found anywhere. We expected the basilica to be busy with tourists, so we made sure to arrive when it opened at 9am. For the most part we had the place to ourselves. The Roman mosaics here are certainly the best I have seen, but the highlight was the dazzling gold mosaics in the domed ceiling of the main church. We climbed to the top of the belltower and walked the ramparts of the complex looking over the sea. You cannot come to Poreč and not see the Euphrasian Basilica.

After this, we walked around the streets and saw more ruins at the Istrian Parliament and admired the facades of many beautiful buildings all over town. Poreč has a very different feel than the romanticism of more Venetian Rovinj but it was equally worth seeing and spending a night there.

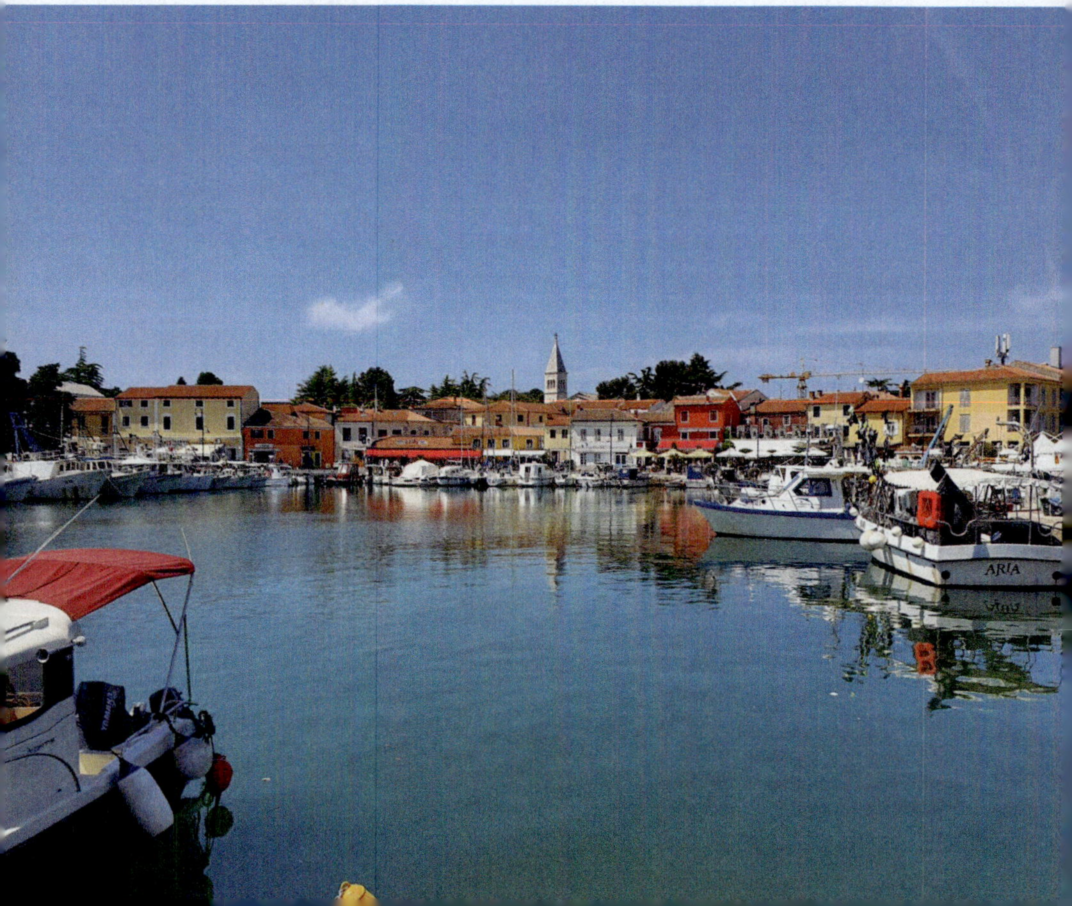
ARIA

Novigrad

This was our last full day in Istria, as our flights back to the UK from Venice Airport were booked for the following day. We had already used up quite a bit of our day in Poreč and had two more places we really wanted to see. It would be a bit of a push, but I wanted to squeeze in Novigrad a little further up the coast before heading inland.

With such an austere-sounding name, I was slightly concerned that this detour might not be worth it. Even the Italian name Cittanova, widely signposted, implied a less traditional Istrian town. But as soon as we arrived and looked at this lovely small walled town across the harbour, we knew we had to explore. This harbour had the highest concentration of fishing boats so far on our trip, which bode well for lunch.

Novigrad is home to three of Croatia's top restaurants, which in turn attract several more top places to eat. We walked around this lovely small town, more a fishing village, and paddled in the sea. We hadn't really had a proper sit-down lunch in Istria and while we were not looking for a long lunch involving a tasting menu, we couldn't walk past all the restaurants any longer. We had a lovely meal at another konoba (Kristijana) sitting at a table under an umbrella to shelter from the midday heat. I bought a bottle of Teran wine from one of the local vineyard shops and we hit the road heading inland.

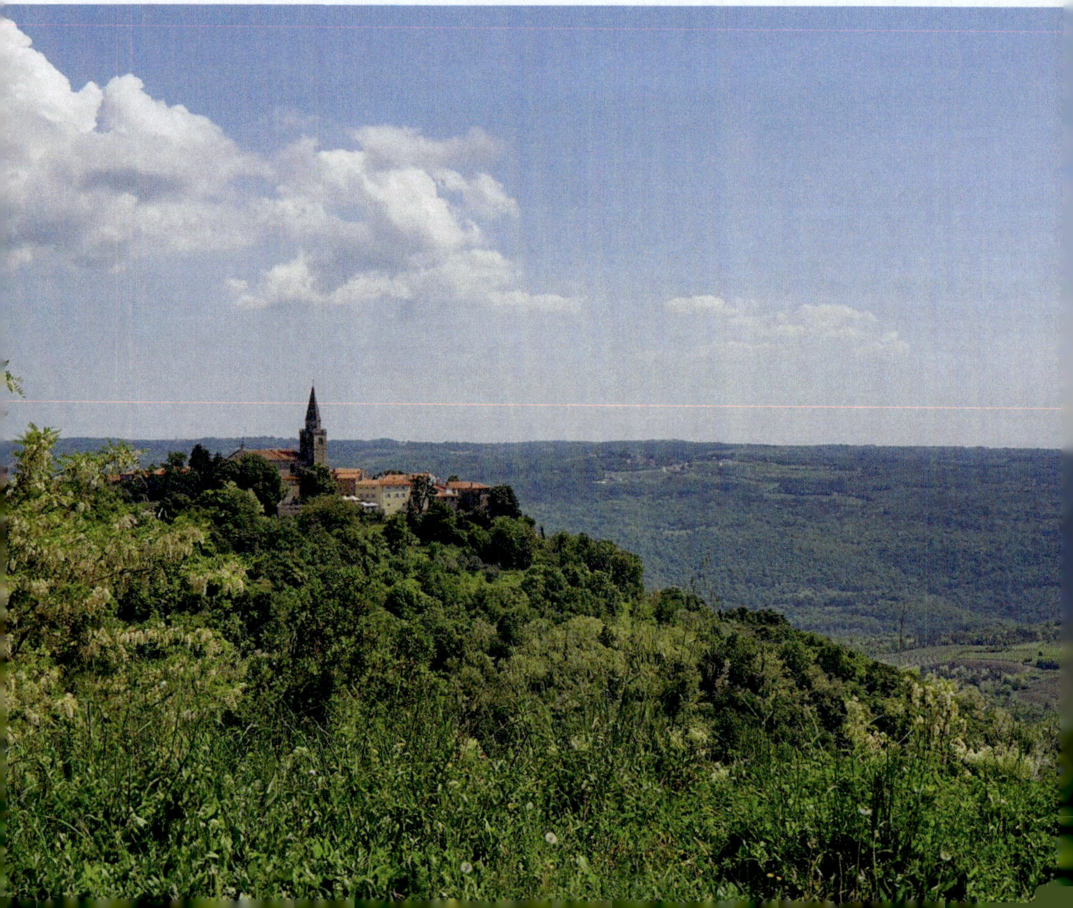

Grožnjan

According to the guide books, the top two Istrian hill top towns to see are Motovun and Grožnjan. We didn't really have time for both and chose Grožnjan because it was smaller and not as far inland. The drive through the hills was stunning, tracking part of the Parenzana road cycling and walking route of "health and friendship". We parked and walked the few hundred metres into the heart of the fortified town. It was like a walk back in time with cobbled streets and vistas across the Istrian countryside. There were some lovely looking restaurants with fabulous views here too. We were in the heart of Green Istria and it was a dramatic change from the Blue Istria we had grown used to.

Grožnjan had an arty feel about it with several galleries and independent craft shops. Emily spent a small fortune in the Zigante truffle shop, where there were pictures of Giancarlo Zigante holding up his prized world record 1.3 kg white truffle, which he found one morning with his dog, not far from the town. Grožnjan is well worth seeing. It is picture postcard pretty almost everywhere you look. It reminded me very much of a hilltop town, Chateaudouble, in Provence where I used to stay with some dear friends.

61

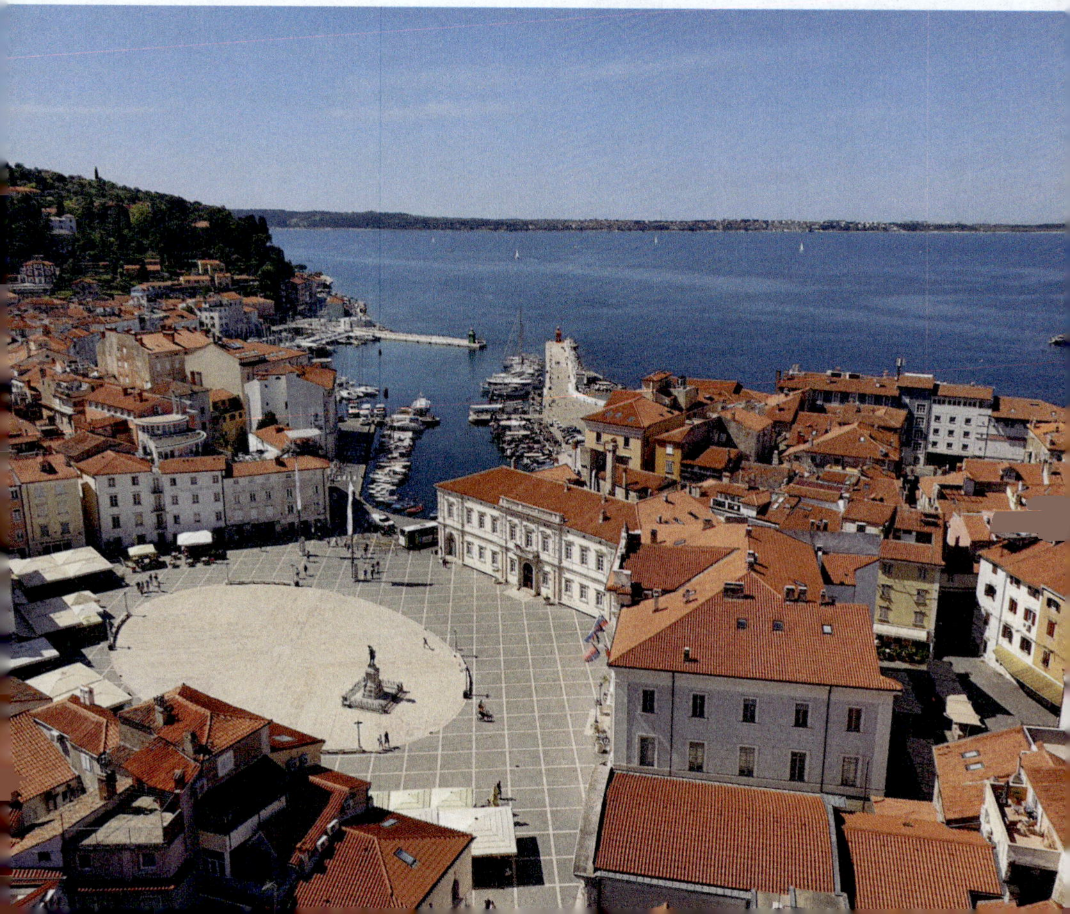

Piran

Twenty minutes after leaving Grožnjan and driving north, you arrive at the border to Slovenia, which Istria extends into geographically. The Slovenian coast along the Adriatic is only 40km long. The main town is Koper with Piran and Izola being the other options for the last night of our trip. We chose Piran, on the basis of convenience for driving and our travel time constraints.

From the Slovenian border the drive takes you down to the coast, past salt pans to Piran at the end of a headland. The town feels even more Italian and is very Venetian, with a tall campanile dominating the town. We checked into the Piran Hotel in pride of place on the waterfront. We had a lovely view of the harbour and across the bay where we could sit on our terrace watching the world go by. It was hot, and a noticeably more humid climate than elsewhere in Istria, so we went for a swim in the sea off the stone jetty right in front of the hotel. Several cyclists of the Parenzana were also ending here; the hotel was clearly used to accommodating cyclists and the sea was undoubtedly a welcome reward following the hills and heat.

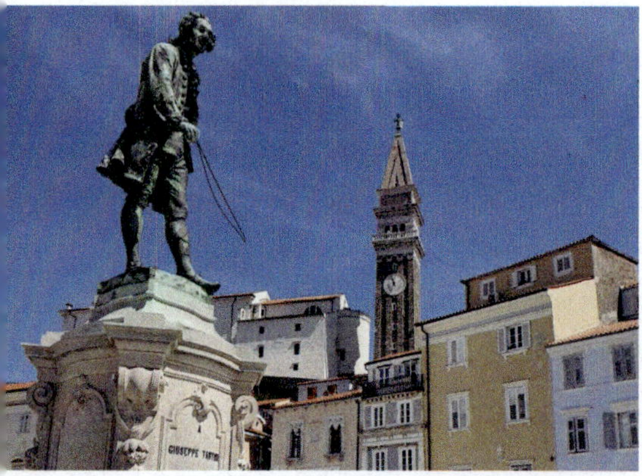
GIUSEPPE

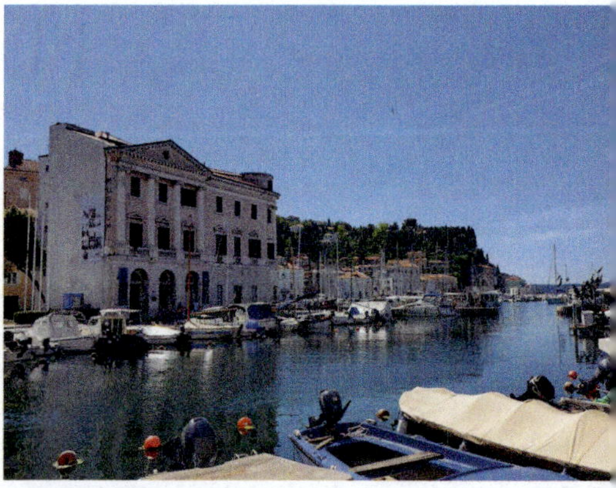

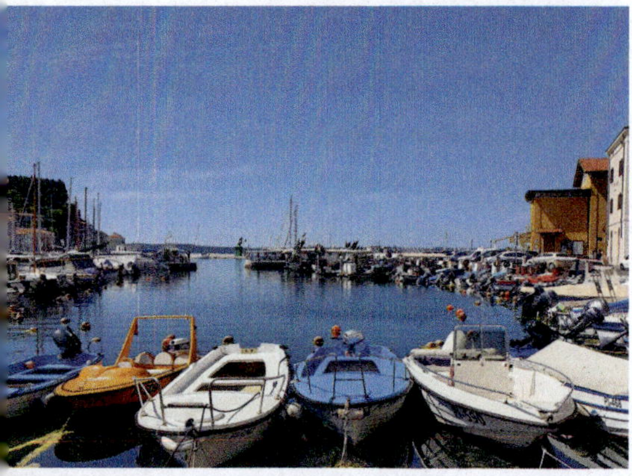

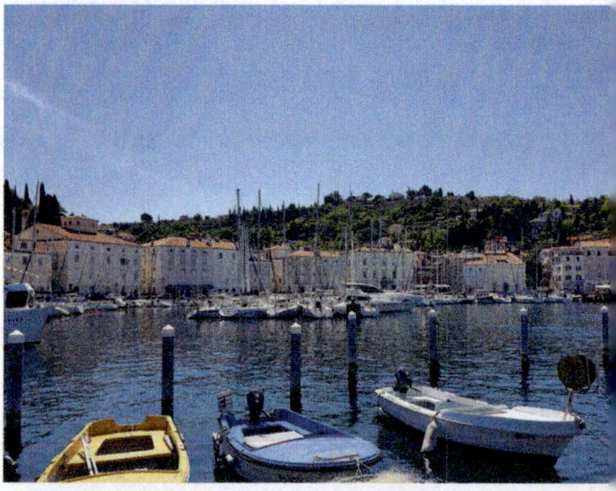

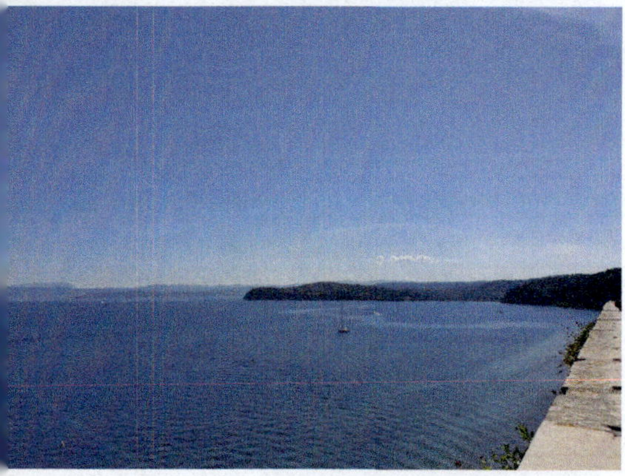

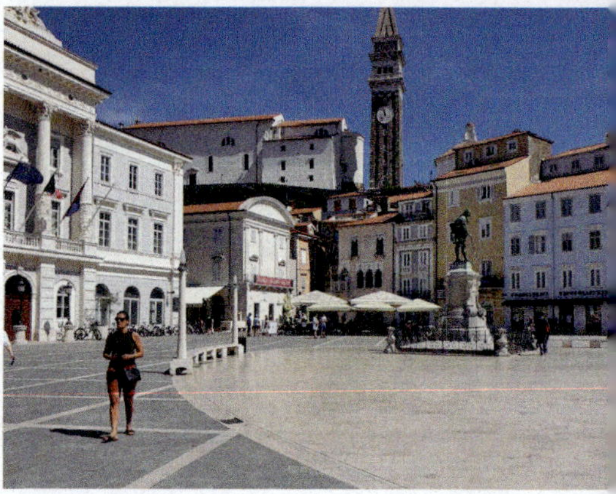

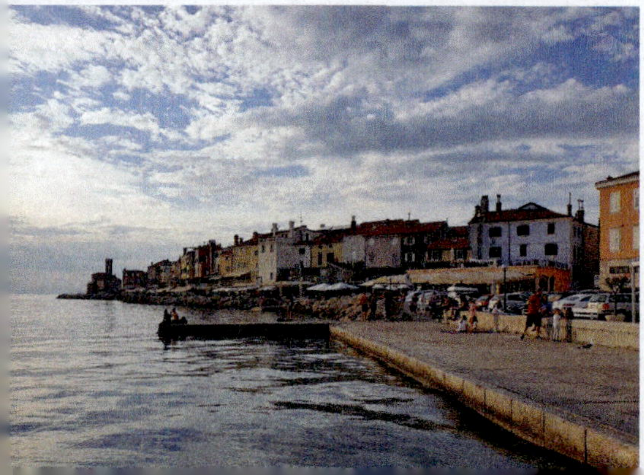

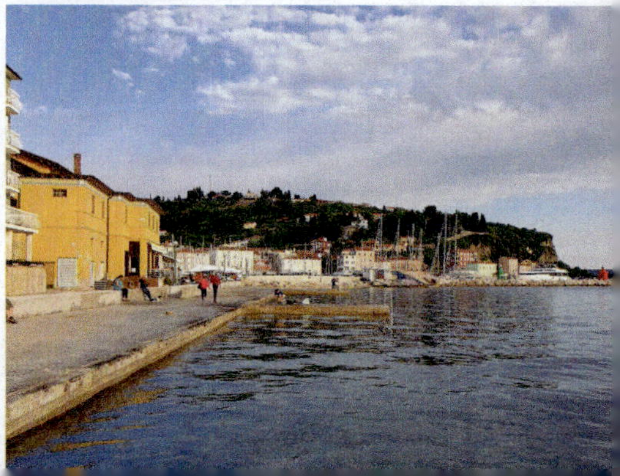

We had booked a restaurant called Neptun (no e) for dinner. Close friends of mine, Craig and Emma, who also know a thing or two about food and wine, had raved about it, describing it as the best seafood restaurant in the world. Quite a claim, so we had to try it. The restaurant is a small family-run place up one of the backstreets off the harbour full of fishing boats. The fish was amazing but the highlight of our meal was a platter of raw scampi or small langoustines. I had been told to try them and to be mindful that the choice of the catch of the day would narrow as the evening progressed. I asked Boštjan, the owner's son who served us, if he had the langoustines and he said 'the day we don't have those is the day we close.' It is hard to describe the fresh taste but it was an unmistakably langoustine taste and if I could always eat them fresh and raw like this, I definitely would.

After dinner, we walked around the harbour and the main piazza – which used to be the harbour until it was filled in in 1884. The square, well it's an ellipse, was renovated with its distinctive white stone in the 1980s. It was lovely at night and on the way home we stopped for a drink and a dance to live music in the small square by the harbour which also doubles up as a morning fish market.

Our last morning was dedicated to walking around Piran. The main thing for us to do was to climb to the top of town of St George's Cathedral. Here you are afforded views all over town, which are further improved from the top of the campanile. We walked the warren of cobbled alleyways and along the seafront where sculptors had carved some of the rocks on the breakwater.

At lunchtime, it was time for us to leave and head to the airport. Driving past, Izola and Koper looked interesting but if you only have time for one place, as we did, Piran is a gem on the Slovenian coast.

We dropped the car off at Venice airport and while we waited at the gate we looked longingly at the Venetian skyline in the distance. It was such an amazing week and given the option to do it all over again from here, I would in a heartbeat.

67

Last Thoughts

It is really hard to say which part of the trip was best. Venice is so iconic and unique that it simply must be visited at least once in a lifetime. I could easily manage a trip there every year, especially with a foray into a neighbouring region such as Istria.

Istria is a complete gem in so many ways and it still feels relatively undiscovered. The scenery is spectacular and the Venetian architecture and cultural influences provide a stunning backdrop. We were not disappointed with any place that we visited. Was a week enough time? Just. You could easily spend two or more weeks in Istria, which would be harder to do in Venice, especially on a budget. This book shows that a lot can be achieved in a week and, if you do plan to visit, it should give you a taste and help with planning your trip.

Perhaps the biggest draw is the amazing range of regional foods and wines. This adventure was our *week in foodie heaven*. Hopefully, it will be yours too.

Guide Book Reviews

Books on Istria

I bought all the books I could get my hands on and read up as much in advance and during the trip. Here is a quick review of each of them.

Bradt Travel Guide – Croatia: Istria with Rijeka and the Slovenian Adriatic

2nd Edition – Published April 2017 – 232 pages

This is most comprehensive and up to date guide on Istria and the one we referred to most. It has a useful map spread over two pages which was great for route planning. And the highlights of what to see in the first few pages and marked on the map leant us towards this guide as our first resource.

The background section at the beginning is well laid out and gives a good brief history of the region in just three pages. There is a Practical Information section as well. Thereafter the book is split into seven regions, starting at the southern tip (Pula being the main draw here) and heading up the more popular west coast, Rovinj, Poreč. The inland part of Istria is covered next followed by the east coast (Opatija) and then Rijeka (not part of Istria proper, we didn't visit). Last of all is the Slovenian Adriatic which we did visit at the end of our trip.

Although this book was a bit big to fit in your pocket, we did have it with us a lot of the time. We referred to it in the car, at breakfast or at lunch.

Time Out Shortlist Guide – Istria

Published 2010 – 192 pages

The great advantage of this guide is that it is a pocket guide and consequently, I nearly always had it in my back pocket each day. The first section was a 'Don't miss this' and roughly aligned with the Bradt guide. The second section, Itineraries, is really good. It covers Wine and Olive routes great page sized maps for each with all the vineyards and olive oil producers marked on. These sections were right up our street. There was a section for Istria by bike, which would be a great way to see it if you had the time. The Time Out Guide covers areas in much the same order as the Bradt guide – West coast, Pula and the south, inland and last just part of the East Coast. Strangely Opatija wasn't covered.

Berlitz Travel Guide – Istria and the Croatian Coast
Published 1977 – 128 pages

Clearly this book was way out of date. It is even smaller than the Time Out guide and covers Slovenian Istria, Ljubljana the Slovenian capital and the Croatian coast around 100 miles south. This was written well before the collapse of Communist Eastern Europe when Istria was part of what was Yugoslavia, which broke up into several countries after the collapse of the Berlin Wall.

The guide is quite interesting for its dated quality and photographs from the seventies. It's thin on the ground and you would easily survive without it.

Istria County – Croatia
Aiden Taylor
Self-Published 2021 – 203 pages – Large Print – no pictures

This book held some promise for me having been written so recently by a self-published author. In fact, the short introduction is quite captivating and I was initially worried that Istria had already been written about in a style I was aiming for. Aiden is American and his clearly spent quite a bit of time in Istria. Sadly, the book starts to become a bit of a ramble without a structure of chapters, clear sections or an index. The order in which things are covered is quite haphazard and some pictures would have helped the text. I ended up skim reading the book and occasionally trying to find bits I had read previously as a sort of guide. It gives a different flavour than a guide book, which is what I am attempting with this book, but it could have been much better. And it doesn't cover Opatija and the main draws of Poreč, Rovinj and Pula are not really written about in any detail.

Istria – Recipes and Stories from the hidden heart of Italy, Slovenia and Croatia.
Paola Bacchia
Published 2021 – 271 Pages – Hardback Cookbook

This lovely cookbook is the book I picked off a bookshelf in Mallorca and it inspired me to turn my trip to a conference into a more focused gastronomic tour of the region. So, I feel a little indebted to this book. You are unlikely to carry this hardback around Istria, but it really is worth perusing the recipes, photos and anecdotes of Istrian cuisine if you are embarking on a gastronomic adventure. It serves as a great backdrop for all the lovely produce and meals you will have.

Monty Don's – Adriatic Gardens BBC iplayer
First aired January 2022 – Three, hour long episodes

This gardens focused series also provided a good deal of inspiration for our trip. The first episode is entirely set in Venice. We visited three of the gardens covered here and were really glad we did. The second episode covered Croatia with reference to the gardens and parks of Opatija, where we spent our first two nights in Istria.

The stand out theme, for me, that came out of this series is that Croatians generally don't garden for the pleasure of gardening as we do in England. Decades of communism and years of relative individual poverty means that there is a deep routed culture of growing food. And it is true that many of the residential gardens we saw were entirely given over to fruit trees and vegetable patches.

As you drive around Istria it is a series of small holdings where the people are more self-sufficient. Every spare patch of land in towns and villages is given over to growing food. You see tiny vineyards and olive groves surrounding modest houses. Had it not been for this brilliant series, I may have taken longer to notice this phenomenon. And it is a big part of why Istria's food culture and the providence of the produce is the bedrock of this amazing region.
Watch it before you go!

I was born on the Mornington Peninsula on Australia's southern coast. My family moved to the UK when I was sixteen and I attained the nickname Dingo, which has stuck ever since. I studied Engineering at Kings College London and have run a software company ever since graduating. When I am not travelling, I live in Cowes on the Isle of Wight in England, where I can mostly be found on or by the sea.

I welcome any questions or feedback at: david@updata.co.uk

I am grateful for a review on Amazon

My other books

Around the World in 80 Countries
Travel Experiences of a Lifetime

Fuerteventura
A winter escape

Cloud Charts
Trading Success with the Ichimoku Technique

Printed in Great Britain
by Amazon